Holy Places

The
Vatican
and Other Christian Holy Places

Victoria Parker

For information, address the publisher:
Raintree, 100 N. LaSalle, Suite 1200, Chicago, IL 60602

Design by Joanna Sapwell and StoryBooks
Printed and bound in China.

07 06 05 04 03
10 9 8 7 6 5 4 3 2 1

Library of Congress Cataloging-in-Publication Data

Parker, Victoria.
  The Vatican / Victoria Parker.
      p. cm. -- (Holy places)
Summary: An introduction to Catholicism which focuses on the Vatican City.
Includes bibliographical references and index.
  ISBN 0-7398-6081-X (HC), 1-4109-0054-1 (Pbk.)
  1. Rome (Italy)--Church history--Juvenile literature. 2. Catholic Church--Italy--Rome--Juvenile literature. 3. Vatican City--Juvenile literature. [1. Catholic Church. 2. Vatican City.] I. Title. II. Series.
  BX1548.R6 R37 2003
  263'.04245634--dc21
                        2002014393

Acknowledgments
The Publishers would like to thank the following for permission to reproduce photographs: AKG Photo p. 11; Associated Press pp. 15, 29; Corbis pp. 6, 8, 27; Corbis/Hanan Isachar p. 20; Corbis/Vittoriano Rastelli p. 28; Corbis/Bettmann pp. 14, 25; Corbis/Charles Lenars p. 26; E & E Picture Library/J Allen p. 19; John Heseltine Imagery p. 24; Jon Davison/Lonely Planet Images p. 23; Link/Orde Eliason p. 21; Popperfoto p. 22; Trip/B Seed p. 18; Trip/H Rogers p. 12; Trip/J Greenberg p. 16; Trip/R Cracknell p. 13; Trip/C Rennie pp. 5, 7, 10; Trip/Viesti Collection p. 17.

Cover photograph reproduced with permission of Carlos Reyes Manzo\Andes Press Agency.

Every effort has been made to contact copyright holders of any material reproduced in this book. Any omissions will be rectified in subsequent printings if notice is given to the Publisher.

Contents

Words printed in bold letters, **like this**, are explained in the Glossary on page 30.

What Is the Vatican?

Vatican City is a place in Rome in Italy. It is not just a city. In 1929, it was made a small country on its own, called a state. Vatican City is so small that it takes only an hour to walk around its borders. It is the home of a man called the Pope. The Pope is the leader of the Roman Catholic Church.

Roman Catholics follow the teachings of a man called Jesus, who lived 2,000 years ago. When Jesus was about 30 years old, he spent three years teaching about God.

Many people came to love Jesus and follow him. But a few powerful leaders didn't like Jesus at all. They killed him by nailing him to a cross. This was called **crucifixion.**

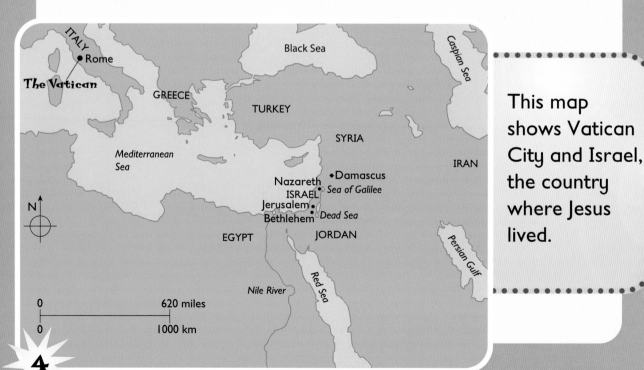

This map shows Vatican City and Israel, the country where Jesus lived.

Many people believe that Jesus came back to life three days after being killed because he was God's Son. These people are called Christians.

There are three main groups of Christians in the world today: Roman Catholics, Protestants, and Orthodox Christians. Roman Catholics are the largest group.

St. Peter's Square lies at the center of Vatican City.

Roman Catholic Headquarters

This famous painting shows Jesus with his closest friends.

Two thousand years ago, Jesus chose one of his closest friends, Peter, to lead all his followers. Roman Catholics call Peter the first Pope. Peter traveled to many countries teaching people about Jesus. He finally settled in Rome.

The Roman **Emperor** Nero hated Christians and eventually put Peter to death by **crucifixion.** Peter was buried on Vatican Hill. Nearly 300 years later, a different Emperor called Constantine became a Christian himself.

What is the Holy See?

The Vatican City is sometimes known as the "**Holy** See." This is another way of saying the seat of Peter. The word "see" means seat in the type of English that was spoken about 1,000 years ago. It is holy because Peter is a saint.

Christians believe that Peter was a very important **saint.** Constantine ordered a **basilica** to be built on top of his **tomb.**

St. Peter's Basilica was rebuilt into a mighty cathedral surrounded by palaces, offices, and gardens. This is the area now known as the Vatican City-State.

This is one of the altars inside of St. Peter's Basilica.

What Is it Like Inside Vatican City?

This summer house is in the Vatican gardens. It was built over 300 years ago.

From inside the Vatican, the Pope is responsible for guiding Roman Catholics all over the world. Around 4,000 people work at the Vatican to help him. Most of these live outside the Vatican's borders, in Italy. This is because the Vatican does not have ordinary houses like other cities. The 1,000 or so people who live there stay in apartments in the palaces and office buildings.

The Vatican has its own supermarket, **pharmacy,** post office, and train station. It also prints a daily newspaper, and has a radio station and a TV station that broadcast all over the world. But there are no hotels, restaurants, schools, hospitals, or traffic lights.

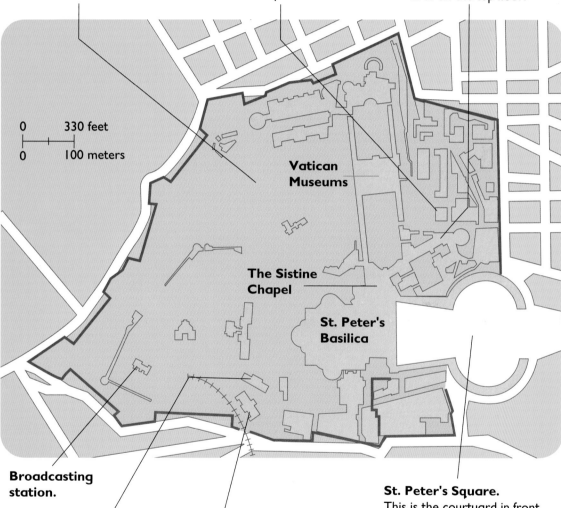

Woods and gardens.
There are many beautiful statues and fountains here. The Galleon Fountain is a boat that shoots water from 16 cannons and some of its masts.

Post Office.
The Vatican prints its own stamps and makes special coins.

The Apostolic Palace
(the Pope's palace).
This is the main building in the Vatican. It has more than 1,400 rooms, nearly 1,000 flights of stairs, and 20 courtyards. The Pope lives on the top floor.

0   330 feet

0   100 meters

Vatican Museums

The Sistine Chapel

St. Peter's Basilica

Broadcasting station.

Mosaic School.
The Vatican makes and sells beautiful **mosaics**.

Railway station.
Trains bring food and other supplies into the Vatican.

St. Peter's Square.
This is the courtyard in front of St. Peter's Basilica. A white line across it marks the border with Italy. On the other sides, the Vatican is closed in by a wall.

Here is a map of the Vatican.

What Is St. Peter's Basilica?

St. Peter's **Basilica** is the biggest church in the world. It is so enormous that more than six football fields would fit inside it. It has 50 **altars,** many **chapels,** and over 400 statues. Over 10 million tourists visit St. Peter's every year.

Christians go to a church to worship God. The **congregation** sit on long benches called pews and pray in front of an altar. Roman Catholics often kneel to pray.

Here is the front of St. Peter's Basilica.

When Roman Catholics go into a church, they dip the fingers of their right hand into a dish of **holy water** and make a cross shape over themselves. This is called the Sign of the Cross. Christians make the Sign of the Cross to show that they are followers of Jesus and to ask God to **bless** them.

They believe that God is in the churches with them. Above the altar hangs an image of Jesus Christ on the cross. This is called a **crucifix**. At the side of a Roman Catholic church, there is a little open room where people can pray to Jesus' mother, Mary. This is called Our Lady's Chapel. Churches are decorated with statues, flowers, and candles.

This statue is called the *Pieta*. It shows Jesus' mother carrying his dead body.

How Do Roman Catholics Celebrate Their Faith?

The night before Jesus died, he shared a meal with his twelve closest friends, the **Apostles.** This is known as the Last Supper. During a service called **Mass,** Roman Catholics remember the Last Supper in a ceremony called Holy Communion. This is their most important ceremony held in a church.

A priest leads the worshipers in saying prayers and singing **hymns.** Then the priest asks God to **bless** bread and wine, just like Jesus did at the Last Supper.

This priest is celebrating Mass in a Roman Catholic church in Britain.

The first sacrament

Roman Catholics believe that there are seven special blessings from God called sacraments. The first sacrament is baptism. Christian babies are usually baptized to welcome them into the religion when they are very young. The priest will name the baby and bless him or her with **holy water.** The baby's parents and **godparents** will promise to teach the baby about the religion as he or she grows up.

Roman Catholics believe that when God blesses the bread and wine, it is turned into the body and blood of Jesus. The priest then shares it with each worshiper.

In St. Peter's **Basilica,** there is an **altar** at which only the Pope celebrates Mass. This is the splendid High Altar. It is positioned directly over St. Peter's **tomb.**

The High Altar is over St. Peter's tomb. An enormous dome rises above it.

Visiting the Pope and His Palace

The Pope and his most important helpers live in the Apostolic Palace. This is a huge building made up of many small palaces built together. The Pope has an apartment on the top floor that faces St. Peter's Square. It has a garden on the roof that is cleverly hidden by trees and plants, so the Pope can walk and pray in private.

Every year, thousands of people come to the Vatican from all over the world to see the Pope. Roman Catholics think it is very special to be **blessed** by him. Every Sunday morning, big crowds gather in St. Peter's Square outside the Apostolic Palace. At midday, the Pope appears at his window and blesses everyone below.

Pope John Paul II blesses the crowd in St. Peter's Square.

Who wears what?

The Pope's closest **advisors** are called **cardinals.** They are in charge of church leaders called **bishops.** The Pope wears white, cardinals wear red, and bishops wear purple. For ceremonies, they all wear a pointed hat called a miter. They also carry a type of shepherd's crook called a crozier, because Jesus said he was a Good Shepherd leading the flock of his people to God.

In the summer, the Pope moves away from Rome to a house in the country called Castel Gandolfo. He gives Sunday blessings here, too.

The Pope also holds regular meetings in the Vatican called **audiences.** Lots of people come to listen to the Pope talk about God. These audiences are often held in St. Peter's Square or in the **Basilica.**

These cardinals and bishops are wearing their special robes.

Why Is the Sistine Chapel Special?

The Pope's palace has its own **chapel,** which was built 500 years ago. It is called the Sistine Chapel. An artist called Michelangelo was asked to decorate the walls and ceiling by painting on them. It took him four years to finish the job.

Michelangelo painted beautiful pictures of stories from the Bible. The Bible is the Christians' **holy** book. They believe it is the word of God. Michelangelo first painted scenes showing how God created the world.

Later, Michelangelo painted the Last Judgement. It shows how God will punish bad people and reward good people at the end of the world.

Michelangelo's paintings cover the entire Sistine Chapel.

Solomon's temple

The Sistine Chapel has another close link with the Bible. The Bible tells about an important **temple** that was built long ago by a **Jewish** king called Solomon. The Sistine Chapel is built with exactly the same measurements as this ancient temple in the Bible story.

For hundreds of years the paintings were slowly getting covered with dust and smoke from the chapel candles, so they became very dirty.

In 1980, experts began to clean up Michelangelo's amazing ceiling. It took the team 12 years to clean away all the grime. Now, the ceiling glows with beautiful colors once more.

The paintings on the ceiling of the Sistine Chapel are famous all over the world.

17

Vatican Treasures

Many people visit the Vatican to see some of the finest treasures in the world. The first display happened 500 years ago, when Pope Julius II put several ancient paintings on show. Other Popes continued to collect works of art and valuable objects. Today, the Vatican Museum in the Apostolic Palace has many rooms full of priceless pictures, statues, jewelry, and **mosaics.**

The museum contains items that are special for Roman Catholics. Many of the statues of the **saints** there are hundreds of years old. There is a gallery of religious works of art by modern artists, too. However, many items at the Vatican Museum do not have to do with Christianity.

Here is a 2,000 year old carving from the Vatican Museum.

Very long letters!

The Vatican library has huge storerooms called archives. These contain letters from important people through history such as King Henry VIII of England, Mary Queen of Scots, and the Italian scientist Galileo. There are so many letters that if you laid the shelves of the Vatican Archives end to end, they would stretch for over 15 miles (25 kilometers)!

Many of the treasures were made by people who lived thousands of years ago in ancient Rome, Egypt, and Greece. There are statues of their gods and goddesses, and sculptures from their **tombs.** There are also ancient mosaics, two Roman **chariots,** statues of Greek poets and heroes, and even an Egyptian **mummy!**

This column was made in ancient Rome. It stands in the center of St. Peter's Square.

Saints and Relics

One of the Pope's duties is declaring people to be **saints.**
A saint is somebody who lived a very **holy** life. Christians
believe that saints are close to God in heaven and can ask
Him to help people on Earth. Only a very few men and
women are holy enough to be given this title.

Roman Catholics believe that some saints, called patron
saints, can give special protection. For example, St. Joan
of Arc is the patron saint of soldiers and French people.

Anything that once
belonged to a saint or
Jesus, such as a piece
of clothing, hair, or
bone is called a relic.

Roman Catholics
believe that this is
a relic of the table
where Jesus Christ
ate his Last Supper.

DID YOU KNOW?

The Pope is now thinking about giving the title of saint to a **nun** named Mother Teresa. Mother Teresa spent her whole life helping very poor people in the city of Calcutta in India. It may take a long time for the Vatican to look at all the evidence and decide.

Roman Catholics think that relics are **sacred.** They are kept safe inside churches. St. Peter's **Basilica** has a veil that people believe Saint Veronica used to wipe Jesus' face when he was on his way to die. There is also a relic believed to be a bit of a spear that a Roman soldier stabbed into Jesus' side after he died.

The most important relic is a piece of wood that people believe is from the actual cross Jesus died on. All these precious relics are put on display at Vatican festivals.

Vatican City has its own army called the Swiss Guards. The soldiers are sworn to protect the Pope.

Feast Days and Festivals

The Pope is blessing pilgrims in St. Peter's Square at Easter.

All groups of Christians celebrate several important festivals. Christmas Day is Jesus' birthday. Many Roman Catholics go to **Mass** at midnight on Christmas Eve to celebrate the birth of Jesus Christ.

The most important festival is Easter. Easter begins on Good Friday, the day Jesus died. Roman Catholics hold a very solemn service in church on this day. There are no flowers and the statues are covered up. Easter Sunday is when Jesus came back to life. There is a joyful Mass on Easter Sunday.

Each Christmas Day and Easter Sunday, the Pope gives a speech called *Urbi et Orbi*, which is **Latin** for "to the city and to the world." Fifty thousand people wait in St. Peter's Square to hear him. His speech is also broadcast on TV and radio. The Pope talks about worldwide events and how God wants people to live. He gives a special **blessing** to all people.

DID YOU KNOW?

Long ago on Good Friday night, the Pope and a rich man both had the same dream. In their dreams Mary, the mother of Jesus, told them it would snow the next day—even though it was summertime!

Mary asked the men to build a church where the snowflakes fell. Everything happened just as she said and the Basilica of St. Mary Major was built in Rome. Every year a beautiful ceremony takes place where white flower petals are scattered around the church.

This is the Basilica of St. Mary Major in Vatican City.

23

Places of Pilgrimage

A story says that St. Peter was once traveling away from Rome along a road called the Appian Way, when Jesus suddenly appeared to him. They spoke to each other. Then Jesus vanished, leaving his footprints on the ground. Later, a church called Quo Vadis was built on the spot. (*Quo Vadis?* is Latin for "where are you going?") Today, many **pilgrims** go there to see two footprints set in stone. People believe that they are the footprints Jesus left behind.

Pilgrims also visit the ancient burial grounds that line the Appian Way. These are called the catacombs. Thousands of early Christians were buried here. Many of them were put to death by the Romans for following Jesus.

The church Quo Vadis is on the ancient Appian Way.

What is a Holy year?

Every fifty years, there is a **Holy** Year for Roman Catholics. The Bible says that God asked for this to happen. Roman Catholics believe that if they make a pilgrimage to the Vatican and Rome in Holy Year, God will grant them special **blessings.** A Holy Year begins with Midnight **Mass** on Christmas Eve when the Pope opens a Holy Door in St. Peter's Basilica. At the end of Holy Year, the door is closed and bricked up.

One Christian who died for his beliefs was a **saint** called Paul. St. Paul's **tomb** is surrounded by a huge church in Rome. It is owned by the Vatican and is called the **Basilica** of St. Paul Without the Walls. Pilgrims travel from all over the world to visit it.

Pope John Paul II opens the Holy Door in St. Peter's Basilica to start the Holy Year.

Other Roman Catholic Holy Places

Jesus lived in Galilee, an old area in the **Middle East,** near the city of Jerusalem, in Israel. Today, Christians make **pilgrimages** to visit the places in which Jesus lived and died.

Many pilgrims go to Bethlehem, where Jesus was born. In Jerusalem, pilgrims walk the path Jesus took through the streets when he carried his cross to be **crucified.** This route is called the Via Dolorosa, which means the Way of Sorrows. The Church of the **Holy** Sepulchre is at the end of the route. Here, pilgrims can see where they believe Jesus was stripped of his clothes and nailed to the cross. At the heart of the church lies the **tomb** in which people believe Jesus was buried, before he rose from the dead.

The Via Dolorosa is the road that Jesus walked down to be crucified.

Many Roman Catholics also visit places where they believe Jesus' mother, Mary, has appeared. Saint Bernadette saw Mary at Lourdes, in France. Many pilgrims believe they have been cured of illnesses by washing in a spring and praying there. Many Roman Catholics believe that Jesus' mother Mary has been appearing since 1981 to six young people in a place called Medugorje in Bosnia-Herzegovina. Thousands of people go on pilgrimages there to pray for peace throughout the world.

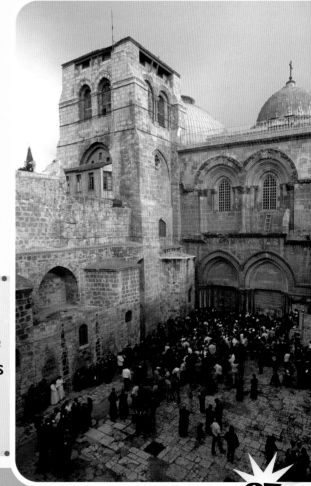

The Church of the Holy Sepulchre is where Christians believe Jesus was crucified.

Who Is Pope John Paul II?

Karol Wojtyla was born on May 18, 1920 in Poland. As a young man, Karol wanted to be an actor. But when **World War II** broke out across Europe, Karol decided to become a priest.

Karol worked extremely hard to help people. He was made a **bishop** and then a **cardinal.** Karol was chosen to be Pope when he was 58 years old. He took the name Pope John Paul II. He was the youngest Pope in over 100 years, and the first Pope to come from Poland.

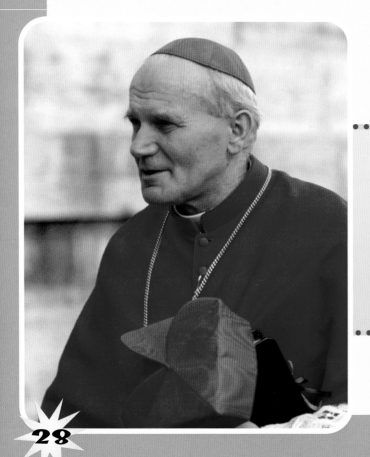

Here is Pope John Paul II when he was still Cardinal Karol Wojtyla.

How is the Pope chosen?

When a Pope dies, the cardinals meet in the Sistine **Chapel** to choose the next Pope from among all the bishops. The cardinals' meeting is called the Conclave. It is top secret. Crowds of people wait in St. Peter's Square. They know when the cardinals have chosen because white smoke is sent up above the Vatican as a sign.

In 1981, a man tried to kill John Paul by shooting him. The Pope was badly hurt and spent three months in a hospital, but he asked God to forgive his attacker. Since then, John Paul has traveled to more countries to meet people than any other Pope. He was also the first Pope to pray in a **Muslim mosque.** He is a very special Pope.

White smoke blows from the chimney of the Sistine Chapel showing that a new Pope has been chosen.

Glossary

advisors   people who help somebody else to make important decisions

altar   table in church that a priest uses during worship

Apostles   Jesus' twelve closest friends

audience   meeting with the Pope

basilica   very old and important church

bishop   important priest who is in charge of a group of churches in an area

bless (blessed)   to ask God to make something holy

cardinal   one of the men whose job it is to help the Pope make important decisions

chapel   side room in a church for worshiping in

chariot   two-wheeled, horse-drawn cart that people in ancient times rode in during races and wars

congregation   people who gather in a church to worship

crucifixion (crucified)   ancient form of punishment when someone was nailed to a large wooden cross and left to die

emperor   ruler of a large area made up of different countries and peoples

godparents   people who promise to teach a child about God as they grow up

holy   to do with God

holy water   water that has been blessed by a priest

hymns   songs sung to worship God

Jews (Jewish)   people who follow a religion called Judaism

Latin   language of the ancient Romans

Mass   main service of worship held in a Christian church

Middle East   area of the world where Jesus Christ came from. It includes the countries Syria, Egypt, Jordan, Lebanon, Israel, and Palestine.

mosaics   pictures made up of tiny pieces of colored glass, stone, or pottery

mosque   building where Muslims go to worship God

Muslims   people who follow a religion called Islam, based on the teachings of a prophet called Muhammad (pbuh)

mummy   dead body from ancient times, which was wrapped up in a special way to stop it from rotting

nun   Catholic woman who has taken a special promise never to get married, but to work for God all her life by living with other nuns, praying, and helping people

pharmacy   place where people can buy medicines

pilgrim   someone who makes a journey to visit a holy place

pilgrimage   journey someone makes to visit a holy place

prophet   person sent by God to teach others how to live good lives

sacred   something believed to be special to God

saint   title given by the Catholic Church to a man or woman who lived a very good life and is close to God in heaven

temple   building where people go to worship God

tomb   stone box that a dead person is buried in

World War II   war from 1939 to 1945 involving lots of countries that started when German armies marched into Poland and took over the country

Index